Ed. James

The complete Handbook of Boxing and Wrestling

Ed. James

The complete Handbook of Boxing and Wrestling

ISBN/EAN: 9783743323346

Manufactured in Europe, USA, Canada, Australia, Japa

Cover: Foto ©Lupo / pixelio.de

Manufactured and distributed by brebook publishing software
(www.brebook.com)

Ed. James

The complete Handbook of Boxing and Wrestling

THE

COMPLETE HANDBOOK

OF

BOXING

AND

WRESTLING;

WITH

FULL AND SIMPLE INSTRUCTIONS

ON ACQUIRING THESE

USEFUL, INVIGORATING, AND HEALTH-GIVING ARTS.

ILLUSTRATED WITH

FIFTY ORIGINAL ENGRAVINGS AND PORTRAITS.

By

ED. JAMES,

AUTHOR OF "THE DUMB-BELL AND INDIAN CLUB," "HEALTH, STRENGTH
AND MUSCLE," "PRACTICAL TRAINING," "MANUAL OF SPORTING

JAMES MACE.

THE SCIENCE

OF

BOXING.

INTRODUCTION.

No one is capable of imparting to others a knowledge of
that which he is not thoroughly familiar with by practical
experience; and those who may out of jealousy or from
inquisitiveness want to be informed as to " What we know
about sparring and wrestling," we will so far gratify as
to say that twenty years or more ago our preceptor was
the renowned Yankee Sullivan, and that later on a regular
course of lessons was had from William Hastings, conqueror of Orville Gardner and others; Sam Freeman, the
best teacher of his day, and James Hunter, of Brooklyn,
who received his tuition from Johnny Walker and Yankee
Sullivan. For a few years we tried to impart all we knew
to a host of others by sparring with them, and while con-
fessing to have received many a sprained thumb, black and
blue arms, and a black eye or two, sprinkled with a few
bloody noses, during our course of sprouts, none of these an-
noyances occurred when possessed of the proper knowledge,
backed up by plenty of practice. Few have witnessed
more glove contests, or oftener acted as referee in matches
with and without the gloves, and had not our sight become
impaired, there is no telling where we should have stopped—

perhaps, instead of dealing in sporting goods and writing books on sporting matters, we might have tacked onto our name "Professor" and been teaching the young idea how to shoot out his left and stop with his right in a proper manner—as we are not, we take this method of giving instruction, believing and hoping all who read, ponder, inwardly digest, and, above all, practice its precepts, may become a great deal cleverer than we ever were.

OBJECT AND BENEFIT OF SPARRING.

THERE is no single exercise taught in our gymnasiums, or practiced on land or water, which calls into active use more parts of the body at the same time than the art of sparring. It brings into play every muscle and nerve from the eyes to the toes, while the brain plays a very conspicuous part. It is for this reason, more than to make candidates for the Prize Ring, we take a stand in its favor, adding that a knowledge of the science will be found of incalculable value if ever you should be forced into a fight, be attacked by some street rowdy, or be called upon to defend either sex from insult or actual assault. A complete knowledge of sparring gives confidence and courage, coolness, presence of mind, quick perception, grace, elasticity, strength, manliness, and, even when the knife or pistol has been attempted to be used, we have known scores of cases where their weapons have been seized and a sound thrashing administered to those bent on killing them or someone else. The main object in sparring is to strike your adversary as often as possible and prevent him from striking you.

GENERAL OBSERVATIONS.

UNTIL you have learned to protect your thumb and got used to guarding, an occasional sprain may be the result, although this need never happen when the hands are properly closed. The right forearm may become more or less bruised, which can be cured by applying brandy and water to the part a few times. In striking, throw the weight of the body on the left leg, bending the knee slightly and extending the right leg as much as possible. In stop-

ping blows, throw your weight on the right leg and always set the muscles of the arm firm, for if kept otherwise, the blow is apt to be the means of making your own arm hurt yourself.

The proper time to strike is when your partner lifts his left foot, or projects his left arm, or shuts his eyes, taking care that he does not initiate by catching you in the same way.

An impetuous sparrer may be very much bothered and annoyed by your simply holding the left arm straight out in front, as he runs at you, receiving its full force in the face, after which he will soon stop to consider and discontinue his rushing tactics.

Straight blows, from the shorter distance they have to travel, compared to round ones, are always the best. We should advise that twenty minutes be the maximum for sparring at one time, as every faculty of the mind and body are actively employed during the set-to, and suggest the propriety of being rubbed dry with a coarse towel at the conclusion. The most dangerous, although not necessarily the most exposed points of attack are the temples, throat, butt of ear, eyes, nose, jawbone, mark (or pit of stomach), loins, ribs and the heart.

It is always best to avoid exercise with the gloves on a full stomach; at least two hours should elapse between eating and sparring, and where possible the set-to should be practiced in a well-ventilated room, or, better still, on the turf in pleasant weather. The costume should be: a short-sleeved undershirt, pantaloons or knee tights, long, white stockings, and high, laced-up shoes with low heels; a handkerchief or web belt tied around the waist, to keep the garments snug, will be found useful. The padding of the gloves should project well over the tips of the fingers, and to avoid what is known as "palming" (striking with the heel of the hand), it would be well to have the gloves heel-padded, with strings to tighten, in order to hold them more firmly on the hand. Medium-sized gloves are the best; those made small and hard are pretty nearly as bad as having none on at all, while the other extreme is to be condemned, it being impossible to make a good display with four pillows between your faces. Gloves when soiled may be cleaned with benzine. As every one, whether with or without lookers-on, naturally wants to appear to the best advantage, it may not be amiss here to state that when sparring where there is sunshine or gas-light, it should be the object to get that light to shine in your rival's face and upon your back.

LEARNING TO STRIKE WITHOUT LOSING BALANCE.

ONE of the first things to be acquired is how to balance yourself, so as in case you miss a blow, not to fall head-long forwards. For this purpose procure a pair of five or six pound dumb-bells, and strike forward at some imaginary object, first left, then right, and so on changing, throwing out the arms full length and as far forward as possible without getting off your balance, keeping the feet in the same position all the time. A striking-bag, fifteen or twenty pounds weight, suspended from above so as to reach about as low as your chest, may be used with great advantage for learning to balance, as well as for hitting out. To acquire celerity of eye, hands, feet and head, suspend an inflated bladder, and hit, parry or dodge as it rebounds—it will keep you busy, and, although recommended by no other work, there is nothing to equal this sparring with the bladder for exercise or amusement.

THE BEST ATTITUDE.

NEARLY every authority as to the attitude of a sparrer differs, but the easiest and most natural position will, by experience, be found to be the best. ..olding the arms high involves a continual strain upon them, more tiresome than their active use. Sawing the air may look showy for a time, afterwards becoming very monotonous as well as useless. Leaning the body forward or backward, standing too wide or too close, are each and all faults very easy to acquire, but hard to get rid of. No better instance, as an example, can perhaps be given than the fighting attitude of Mr. James Mace, the retired champion, who is, beyond a doubt, the cleverest sparrer in the world. (See portrait.)

The head should be held neither too far back nor too far forward, with chin neither too high nor to low, but as natural as possible, without any studied or affected air. Mouth should be closed, and eyes not open too wide—the eyes being the tell-tales; and you should show no intentions with them yourself while practicing, at the same time read-

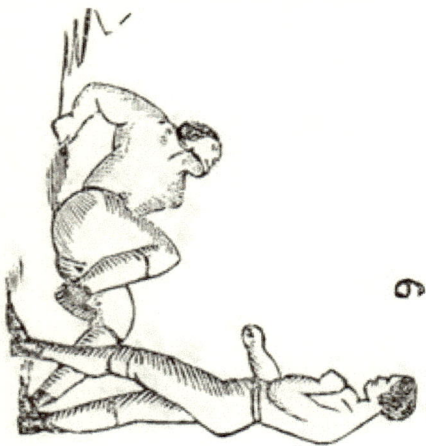

6

5

4

ing your adversary's—only keep a determined look, and don't shut your eyes at every feint or when hit, as this is fatal to you, and just what your opponent wishes. The left arm should be held with the elbow touching a little above the left hip, the forearm slightly curved upwards, the back knuckles to the front, hands partly closed when sparring, wholly so when delivering a blow. The right arm's most natural and proper place is across the body, the hand just below the left nipple and forearm protecting the "mark," or pit of stomach, the inside part of the glove lying flat on the body; the left leg foremost, a little in advance of the right, the latter being turned out more than the former, the weight of the body principally on the right leg. In sparring, throw out your left slightly in advance to and fro, as also your right, but not so much as the other, rising up on the toes, or taking small steps in front when the body should lean slightly toward your man. On stepping forward with your left foot, if he moves backward, bring up your right foot after it; but if he advances, stand your ground, or take a slight back-step, and thus keep manœuvring till you see your chance to lead or counter.

FIRST LESSON.

LEADING WITH LEFT AND STOPPING WITH RIGHT.

In practicing the first movement, the contestants should, in the attitude previously explained, stand near enough for the left-handed straight blow to reach the face, but not so close as to touch each other's feet, and then strike quickly and with full force a straight blow with the left hand at the nose, eye or mouth of each other, always having a point to hit at, and that a vulnerable one, for the forehead or cheek-bone is as much apt to hurt the one striking as the one struck. When one leads, which should be done alternately, the other should stop by either catching the blow on the right forearm, or turning it aside by raising the right arm and throwing the blow one side upwards, but not throwing the hand to the right beyond the line of the shoulder. After the lead, which let go with full force, draw left arm quickly back to the side. Practice this lesson till both can stop and lead well, and without awkwardness or embarrassment.

SECOND LESSON.

LEFT-HANDED COUNTERING.

In the first lesson instruction was given about leading and stopping; this lesson is on leading and stopping at the same instant. No change is necessary in position, but simultaneously each one must dash out his left hand at his opponent's face (always aiming for a special mark), and at the same time raise the right arm, catching the blow as before stated, drawing left back, and repeating the lesson ten or fifteen minutes at a time. When thorough in this movement, but not till then, the back-handed chopping blow, and a very severe one it is, may be used after stopping the left lead, by quickly striking downwards with your right at an opponent's nose before he can recover his proper guard.

THIRD LESSON.

LEADING AND STOPPING LEFT AND RIGHT.

The learners will, in same posture as previously, take it in turns, striking the left at face and right at butt of left ear and stopping these blows. The left must be aimed at the head, a straight hit, followed immediately by the right sent slanting across, the spot in view being the butt of the ear. The manner of stopping these left and right handers is by elevating the right forearm, so that the elbow points upwards, while the right open hand is held over the left ear, leaving room to see over the guard—the first, or left-handed blow, aimed at the head, is thus caught on the right elbow, and the slanting right-hander is stopped by the palm of the other's right. In stopping these blows, the left is held in reserve during friendly practice.

FOURTH LESSON.

STOPPING AND DELIVERING BODY-BLOWS.

No change in figure from other lessons, but instead of leading with left at the face and following with right on ear, the left is directed in a straight line at the pit of the stomach, and the right aslant at the small ribs on the left side. The first, or stomach left-hander, is stopped by knocking the blow downwards with your right, and the

second, or blow at the ribs, must be rendered futile by drawing the left arm over them and close to your side. The stomach-blow is also stopped by keeping the right forearm across it, as in the original guard, which is perhaps the best, as if, in attempting to knock the blow downwards, the movement is made too quick or too slow, you are more apt to be hit than when keeping the arm steady across the body. The pupils can practice delivering the right at the "mark" and the left at the right ribs, which must be stopped by holding the right arm close to the side and knocking downwards with the left. When a blow is aimed at the "mark," and by any mishap it cannot be stopped, drawing in and holding the breath will neutralize the pain otherwise sure to follow.

FIFTH LESSON.

DELIVERING AND AVOIDING CROSS-COUNTERS.

The right-handed cross-counter is only used when the left of your antagonist is on its way to strike and his body thrown somewhat forward by the movement. When his left face-hit is sent out, throw your head slightly to the right, bring the right shoulder forward, and with the right hand aim a slanting blow at his left ear. This cross-counter may be stopped by quickly covering the point of attack with the right hand palm towards your adversary, the same as explained in the third lesson. If you should happen to spar with a man standing right hand and right foot foremost, it will be well to become accustomed to changing your attitude in the same way—the cross-counter then would come from your left sent in over his right lead.

SIXTH LESSON.

UPPER-CUTS.

When an opponent has a habit of ducking his head and thereby avoiding blows without resorting to stopping, it is apt to confuse; but, on a few repetitions, his caper will be made known by certain signs beforehand, which, when properly understood, will give the opportunity to administer that severe blow, the upper-cut, delivered the instant your opponent ducks his head down, by describing a half-circle upwards with the right—if aimed well, with the large knuckles upwards, it will be sufficient to make him quit and stand to you, face to face. Ducking is frequently done to get in on the body, and mostly resorted to by experts, who depend on quickness of legs to get away from the upper-cut. When an opponent attempts to use the upper-cut blows with either hand, by keeping the right arm across the body and the left across the face will form an effectual guard against it.

SEVENTH LESSON.

Ducking and Dodging.

This should only be indulged in when blows are sent in too rapid to stop, as in half-arm hitting, and requires great activity and long practice to adopt with safety. It may be practiced by each one in turn in close quarters, when in a regular set-to, each on his merits, as also dodging the head from side to side. It is fair, and adds much to the interest when all the points are made in a set-to, always looking out and being on the alert for upper-cuts. Dropping on one knee is sometimes resorted to, to avoid a wicked blow when it cannot be stopped or dodged.

EIGHTH LESSON.

Half-arm Hitting.

When in close quarters, or to avoid being taken hold of, or thrown, it is necessary to acquire the half-arm hits, which are those from the elbow to the fist, only needed when there does not admit of striking the full length of arm blow. It will often happen, by accident or unavoidable causes, that you are rushed in upon before being prepared, and that is the time to bring into play all the half-arm hitting you are capable of, which, when an antagonist is retreating, may enable you to literally fight him down.

9

11

NINTH LESSON.

FEINTS.

Almost any trick resorted to to throw an opponent off his guard is a feint. Looking at one place and striking at another is often done—this is not alone a source of perplexity to the amateur, it is almost as much so to the professional till he has got the hang of it. When two are sparring together, one may feint or make believe to aim at the face and send in a stinging hit on the "mark," or feint at the body and with the same hand strike the nose. The left is used almost exclusively in feinting. A steady guard, coolness, and quickness will soon put a stopper on these feints, by being ready to counter or cross-counter when the real blow comes.

TENTH LESSON.

SHIFTING OR MANŒUVRING.

By the time the scholar will have learned this part of the art he will be able to make a good display with a good sparrer. The manœuvring consists of taking back steps to avoid a rusher, or working forward to follow up a retreater, or stepping to the left or right and letting an opponent pass by headlong, administering a cross-counter as he passes, pretty sure to take effect and perhaps knock him down. It is good for both to resort to this, as it will learn to keep a proper balance, one of the great essentials in a good boxer. When about to be cornered, or expecting to be, a step back or wheeling around by throwing the right leg behind the left will enable the party to see how the land lies behind him, so as to avoid a rusher who may be his superior in strength.

ELEVENTH LESSON.

FIBBING.

After a number of exchanges have taken place on both sides, and upon getting into too close quarters, seize your opponent quickly with the left and encircle your arm round his neck, and then fib away at his face with your right. The recipient will reciprocate by fibbing you in return ou the ribs with his right. The way of getting out of the dilemma is to suddenly duck the head, which will release his hold, and then spring back and recover guard.

TWELFTH LESSON.

GETTING IN AND OUT OF CHANCERY.

As in fibbing, explained in the previous lesson, the object is to seize your adversary around the neck with your left arm, drawing his head close to your left side, then putting on the hug by tightening the left arm about his neck, and at the same time holding his left wrist with your left, proceed to punish him about the face with your right until you are tired. To extricate yourself from a similar dangerous condition, if you should fail to induce him by a vigorous use of your right from behind on his short ribs, then force your right arm over his left shoulder against his throat, pressing it backward with all your strength, or make the best of your way by slipping through his arm and dropping on your knees. Another method of getting an opponent in chancery is when he attempts to dodge under either arm, for the purpose of avoiding your lead and to be able to use his fists on you from the rear, to seize him around the neck as he stoops to pass by, and then, holding his head tight, pay him off by a vigorous application about his body, with an occasional rap on the face from behind across your back.

ILLUSTRATIONS.

12

13

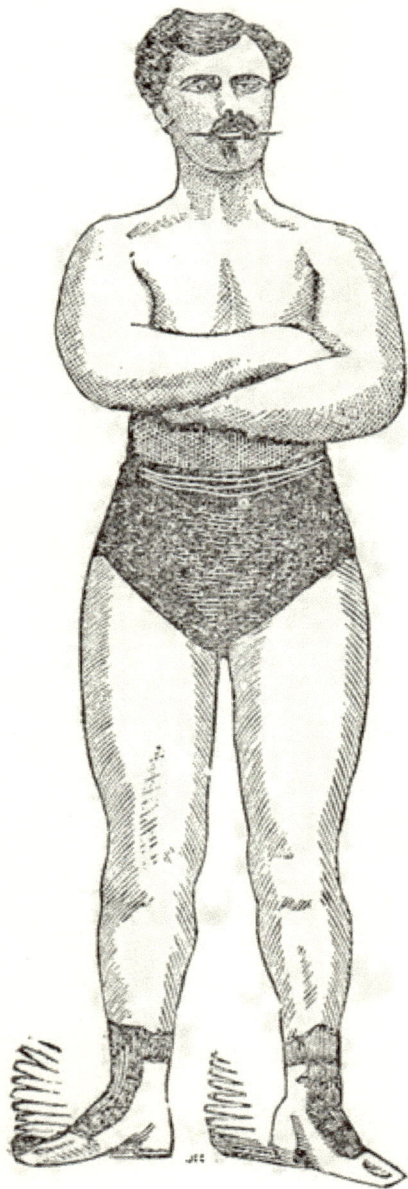

PROF. WM. MILLER.

THE ART

OF

WRESTLING.

GENERAL REMARKS.

Both with regard to security and agreeableness, a close soil, covered with good green turf, is the most proper ground for wrestling on, when care has been taken to remove all the hard bodies which might injure the wrestlers in case of falls, or during the struggles which take place on the ground. Too hard a soil presents but little resistance to the feet, and it weakens the confidence of the wrestlers, because they are afraid of slipping and of hurting themselves in falling. Ground covered with a deep sand is very disagreeable, because in wrestling upon it the body is almost always covered with and the eyes full of sand. Neither boots with high heels, nor shoes with iron about them, should ever be worn while wrestling. The pockets should always be emptied of all things that might be injurious to the movements, or that might do harm at the time of falling. The sleeves of the shirt ought to be turned up above the elbows, the waistband of the trowsers should not be very tight, and the shirt collar should be open. It is expressly forbidden in wrestling for one to take his antagonist by the throat, or by any other improper part, to employ either the nails or the teeth, or

27

to strike him under the chin to make the water come in his mouth.

In wrestling upright the great advantage consists partly in following attentively all the movements of the feet of our adversary, in order to profit by the moment when he makes a false equilibrium; or, when all his forces are not acting in the same way, he fails in his attempt or attack, and gives us, himself, a real advantage. We see by this how useful it is, in order to wrestle with advantage, to study the equilibrium during the active station, then to know how to employ with advantage the action of the lever, to conquer or to oppose any obstinate resistance when our adversary is stronger than we.

The position which sometimes appears hopeless is often that which procures the victory. The reason of it is simple; he who has apparently the advantage almost always abates his vigor, instead of which he who is ready to yield assembles all his powers, makes a last effort, and takes advantages of his adversary, who believed himself already conqueror. The latter is so much the more disconcerted because he did not expect this vigorous resistance; for this reason, he who has the advantage ought never to give himself up to too much security; nor ought he who finds himself in a critical position to despair of success; but, on the contrary, he ought to oppose an obstinate resistance to the last extremity. It sometimes happens in wrestling that he who meets with a vigorous opposition, which he did not expect, soon loses his courage; the violence of the first shock is often followed by a dejection which he is not able to overcome, and the obstinate resistance which he experiences having soon exhausted his strength, he gives up his hopes, sometimes at the very moment when his adversary is on the point of yielding him the victory. As it is seldom that all the qualities of a good wrestler are found united in the same person, the great advantage at the time of the encounter is to discover immediately the weak part of one's adversary; has he the advantage over us with regard to weight, address, prudence and quickness will powerfully serve to fatigue him. (Address doubles the faculties of the body. Prudence and quickness often supply the place of strength when we know how to employ them with advantage.) We must carefully avoid being held tight in the arms of a man who is stronger than ourselves, and being carried away by him,

or we must render his so doing useless and fatiguing by
interlacing ourselves in his legs, and by fixing ourselves
round his neck, which we hold with force. The wrestler
will at length be persuaded that the strength of a man is
of little consequence when he who possesses it is deficient
in those qualities which are acquired by experience and
judgment.

SQUARING WITH THE HANDS, OR WRESTLING WITH THE FISTS.

IN this position he who proposes to drag away the other
ought to assemble all his forces, feel his equilibrium on
the leg which is behind, bend himself gently, place his feet
sideways (or pinch with the sole), and pull strongly that
way which he wishes to bring his competitor. He who
resists employs the same means till he loses his footing.
If the greater force with which he is drawn away hinders
him from stopping himself in a direct line, he makes a pace
sideways, from the right to the left, for example (when the
right leg is forward), draws, by this change of direction,
his partner out of equilibrium, and endeavors to drag him
away in his turn or regain his footing.

HEAD TO HEAD.

IN this style of wrestling the one endeavors to make the
other give way by pushing him strongly with his head and
his arms, one above and the other below. If the ground
is firm both have an equal advantage, which they will not
always preserve, for one will be able, either by strength or
address, to make his adversary recede; and, after he has
once been able to put him in motion, he will never give
him time to regain his footing.

THE BENDING.

IN this action, where perseverance may often procure the
victory, it is forbidden to touch one another with the
hands, or to endeavor to make one let go by throwing him
down, or by wringing his fingers. The bending ought to

be strong enough to hinder the prisoner from escaping,
without, however, injuring him or making him fall down.
The great advantage is to manage our strength, and to
follow, with the greatest suppleness, all the movements of
him whom we hold.   When the prisoner is taller than the
other, the latter ought to raise himself as much as possible
on his toes, to keep up his shoulders, and to force away
the hand which the other tries to introduce by his forearm.
If, after having made several attempts, the prisoner is not
able to disengage himself by introducing one or both arms
between his own body and that of his antagonist, he ought
to take advantage of the moment when the other forces
away the arm which he tries to introduce, and endeavor to
turn himself in the following manner: by leaning himself
to the right, in order to introduce his left arm as soon as
he feels that the other raises his shoulder, he makes a
movement backward with his head, raises his arms paral-
lel to his ears, and throws them forcibly, from right to
left, over the head of his adversary. If he does not en-
tirely succeed in turning himself by this movement, he
leans his right forearm strongly against the nape of the
neck of him who holds him, and remains in this position
till he is able to turn and then disengage himself. He
may also disengage himself without the assistance of his
arms, but for that he must be very strong, and able often
to repeat that blow he makes with his loins, to turn himself as above indicated, or to fatigue the opponent in some
manner or other.

BENDING UPWARDS.

As soon as the engagement begins, he who makes the
attack lowers gently the right hand of his antagonist,
drawing it towards himself, and seizing the moment when
the elbow of the arm, which he lowers, is close to the hip,
he vigorously moves it off with the right, lowers the left
hand of his adversary, making it pass before the body, and
·bends his left arm on the right, by acting strongly with
the shoulder. The two arms are then joined together.
During these different actions, the knee, which is before,
ought to act in concert with the hands, in order that he
who is pulling the other towards himself may make him
lose his equilibrium. Here, the left knee being forward, it
is the right arm which lowers, and the left which moves off

4

and bends. To execute this exercise with advantage requires more suppleness than strength. It contributes powerfully to the development of the breast and shoulders, it fixes the upper part of the body on the hips, and prepares the members for all the fine movements of wrestling.

FORMING THE LEVER.

HERE strength and tallness give one man great advantage over another who is shorter and weaker. However, the victory is not always on the side of the strongest. Here it is the left that bears away, the right and the head press down on the same side; that is, the left arm of the strongest moves away the right of the weakest, at the same time he leans his head strongly against that of his rival, and tries to overthrow him, by holding him always in the same position. This action, making him who is the least and the weakest bend the upper part of his body upon the hips, makes him yield in spite of himself. This movement is composed of four different actions: 1st, that of the left arm, which removes the right; 2d, that of the head, which leans with force in the same direction; 3d, that of the right arm, which pushes down the left shoulder; 4th, the general action of the upper part of the body, which acts to the right, and causes a gentle but almost inevitable fall.

He who proposes to resist this attack lowers himself gently, till he is able to seize, with his lower hand, the leg of his opponent, pull it up with force, put immediately one of his legs behind that on which the other stands, and lean the upper part of his body forward. However little address one may have, with great quickness he will always overthrow his adversary. Or as soon as the weakest perceives that the other wishes to press him down, he moves his head back quickly, interlaces at the same instant his right leg with the left of his antagonist by placing it inside, lifts up forcibly the leg which he holds, and pushes vigorously to the right, with his right arm, which he places across the chin of the other party; if he does not succeed to overthrow him, he ought at least to take advantage of this action to supplant him whom he holds round the body, by raising him from the ground to overthrow him to the right or to the left, without forgetting, especially, the action of the legs.

THE SEVEN SNARES OR TRIPS.

AMONG the great number of attacks used in Greek wrestling, we will point out the seven principal trips, or snares. It is extremely advantageous to understand them well, in order to employ them in case of necessity, or to know how to avoid them.

1st. The first, which is called exterior, is made from right to right, outwards, the knees and the hips kept well together; that is, the leg is placed outwards behind the right of the other man.

2d. From left to left. The left leg outwards, behind the left of the other wrestler. In the first case, the left hand of him who attacks draws back the upper part of the body whilst the right shoulder presses forcibly on the breast of him who is to be overthrown. In the second case it is the right hand which draws, and the left shoulder which presses vigorously. In the warmest moment of the action he who attacks ought to stiffen as much as possible the knee which makes the lever. In either case he who attacks ought to make all these partial movements as one single action, executed with the quickness of lightning; he who resists has the same chance as he who attacks, when he has foreseen the blow soon enough to ward it off; if, on the contrary, he has been surprised, or has no confidence in his strength, he ought immediately to disengage his leg and place it behind.

3d. One may also interlace the right with the left, placing it inside, then the under part of the knees are joined, and he who attacks makes the hook on the fore-part of his rival's leg with the point of his foot.

4th. With the right against the left, in the inside, as above said.

5th. By letting himself fall to the left, to raise quickly from the right, with the top of his foot, the left leg of his adversary, tacking it under the calf, and to make it fall on his back, pulling him with the left hand, at the same time pushing vigorously with the right. In both cases he who is overthrown is made to describe a sort of half-turn on the heel of the foot which rests on the ground.

6th. To fall to the right by lifting up from the left, as above indicated.

7th. By giving a violent push from left to right; to take advantage of the moment when the opponent staggers; to

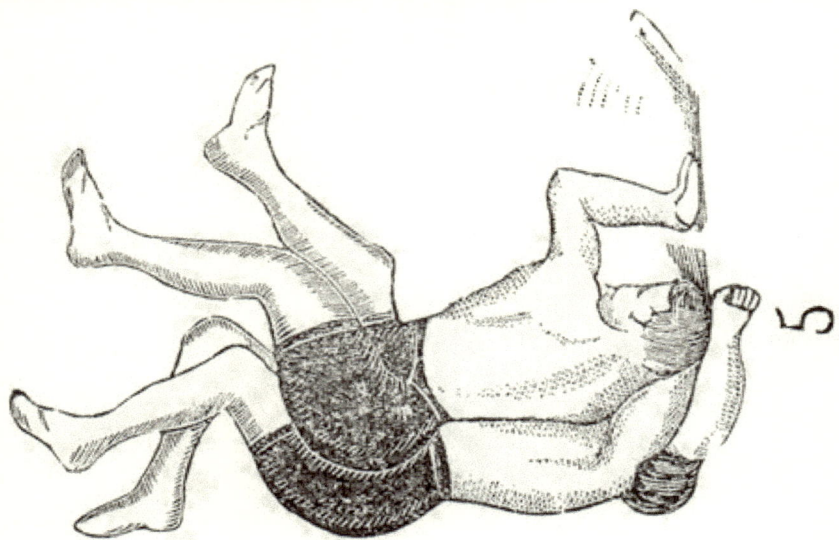

5

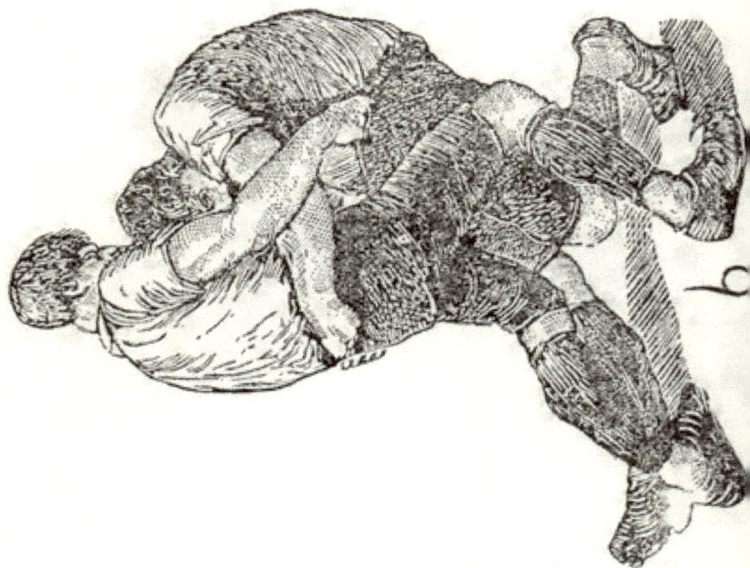

6

place the end of the right foot quickly on the exterior part of the foot of the opposite party, and to push vigorously from right to left, without moving the foot which holds. The exterior snare of the left against the right, and of the right against the left, is given when the adversary presents to us one of his legs, sometimes to make a trap, the right for example. If we see that he intends the exterior snare, from the right against the right, we move the left leg quickly, outwardly, behind that which he presents, by engaging him under the knee, we raise it up, drawing towards us with great force and rapidity; we pull at the same time towards us with the left hand, while we push forcibly with the right. When this action is well executed we seldom fail to overthrow our adversary. The blow of the knee is given at the moment when the adversary, bending backwards, moves one of his legs forwards to overturn you, you seize the instant when one of your knees is behind his, to give him with the knee a strong push in that part, and with your hands you draw or push his body in a contrary way. Care must be taken not to give the blow of the knee, except the knee which presents itself is a little stretched.

TAKING THE ADVANTAGE.

As soon as you have seized your adversary you must press your hand flat against his breast, and raise up your shoulders as much as possible, in order to prevent all his movements. This action takes place standing. The wrestlers place themselves one pace distant from each other, the arms bent, the elbows close to the sides, the fists shut, and crossed one upon the other, as high as the stomach. At a signal agreed on they approach, seize, escape, and let go each other, often several times, with great quickness, and endeavor, by means of all sorts of deceptions, to seize a favorable moment for taking the advantage, each one trying to introduce his arms between the arms and body of his opponent, and to embrace him with sufficient force to preserve the advantage. It is not sufficient only to have seized the adversary, as above indicated, but he must be held in this position till he acknowledges his defeat.

OF THE FIRST FALL.

Sufficiently prepared by all the elements of wrestling, we may now, without fearing any accident, familiarize ourselves with one of the most complicated exercises, both by the variety of the movement and the different situations in which we are placed during the action, which is about to be described. Placed opposite to each other, as has been indicated in the preceding exercise, the wrestlers endeavor, by all sorts of movements, to take the advantage; but as here the principal object is for one to throw down the other, it is permitted in the attack, in endeavoring to take him round the body, to throw him in any manner whatever, and when one of the wrestlers is much quicker and more dexterous than the other, it might happen that the victory may be decided before either has taken this hold of the other, for he who has twice thrown his adversary on his back ought to be acknowledged conqueror. As soon as one has taken the other round the body, he who has obtained the advantage ought to keep his head as close as possible on the highest of his shoulders, in order to hinder his opponent from taking it under his arm; then, in raising him from the ground, to push him from one side and to throw him from the other, or to take advantage of the moment when he advances one of his feet and to throw him down artfully by giving him a trip up. He who loses the advantage ought quickly to move his feet backwards—to lean the upper part of the body forwards—to seize, if possible, the other's head under one of his arms—to fix his other hand on the hip, or on the loins, and to make his adversary bear all the weight of his body.

WRESTLING ON THE GROUND.

In this exercise the two wrestlers are lying on the ground, one on his right side and the other on his left, two feet apart and opposite to each other; their arms are lying on their breasts, or extended down by their sides. The action begins at a signal agreed on, and he who is first able to suspend all the movements of his adversary, by holding him confined under him, upon his back, is conqueror. Here cunning, suppleness, agility, strength, and especially resistance, are indispensable. When the wrestlers are of

nearly equal strength, the victory remains sometimes undecided; each takes his turn to be on the top, and it sometimes happens that he who loses the first part gains the
other two; or, by making an equal part, renders the victory
undecided. In this manner of wrestling, as well as in the
others, they very often engage three times, for it often
happens that he who has the advantage in the first action
loses it in the second, and is consequently obliged to begin
again in order to decide the victory.

SIDE-HOLD THROW.

THROW your right arm around your antagonist's waist, be-
neath his left arm, seizing his right hand with your left in
front, then throw your right leg to the farthest extent behind and towards his right side. Lift him off the ground
by means of the right arm and press the thigh of your
right leg against his left hip, raise your knee, and by a sud-
den jerk throw him backwards. When you do not wish
to struggle, either to avoid being thrown or to throw your
opponent, let your dead weight hang on him and swing
with his movements. By this means you can rest yourself
and tire him out.

BACK-HEEL THROW.

IN giving this fall twist your right heel back and round
your opponent's left heel, right arm across his throat, and
left thrown round his waist under the right arm, clasping
him around the waist. Push forward with your right arm,
draw his body towards you with the left, and by a quick
move of the right leg raise his left foot off the ground and
throw him on his back. To counteract this manœuvre, he
should remove his leg from before yours, thus placed to
entrap him, and place it behind, by which means he obliges
you to stand in the same dangerous situation.

CROSS-BUTTOCK THROW.

RUSH in and grasp the opposite party round his neck with
your right arm, throwing your body across him in front,

seizing his right arm with your left.   Get his body across your hip, and by a violent forward movement of your right shoulder and right hip throw him forward on his head.

COLLAR-AND-ELBOW THROW.

In the square hold, or collar-and-elbow throw, each man shall take hold of the collar of his opponent with his right hand, while with the left he must take hold of his elbow. The men then make play with their legs and try to trip one another by quick movements of their feet, and when either one is off his balance seize the opportunity and twist him over on his back.

JAPANESE THROW.

It is common for the Japanese who desire to become very expert to get their companions to bend back their limbs in constrained attitudes, and thus leave the wrestler for hours and hours together, and, indeed, in some instances, even to dislocate and reset any particular limb.   Bundles of manilla tied up in lengths of about two feet each form the ring, which is laid on the ground.   If the wrestler is thrown within the ring, or falls upon any portion of it, or disturbs any part thereof with his foot, he is considered vanquished.   The wrestlers have to stand back to back, and the appointed judge fastens a cord to the elbow of one and the knee of the other; sundry evolutions are then ordered by the judge, calculated to bring the greatest strain upon the limbs of the wrestlers.   If either of the wrestlers falter under this exercise, frequently painful, he is excluded from the ring and the other declared victor.

ILLUSTRATIONS.

www.ingramcontent.com/pod-product-compliance
Lightning Source LLC
Chambersburg PA
CBHW032136080426
42733CB00008B/1095